# I Got It! Why Not Use It?

By Emmanuel Simms

**FROM THE CREATIVE MIND OF EMMANUEL SIMMS**

Copyright © 2022 Emmanuel Simms
All rights reserved.
ISBN: 9798364389282

**I GOT IT WHY NOT USE IT?**

## DEDICATION

Dear Future, Me,

I am addressing this book to encourage you have a fascinating destiny. I need you to know that I believe in you, and I know you can accomplish all you set your mind to.

I want you to remember that you are capable, and worthy of love and respect. I want you to always stay true to yourself and never give up on your dreams.

I know the world can be tough, but I also know that you have what it takes to make it through anything. Future me, I believe in you. You can do it.

Sincerely,

Your Past Self

**FROM THE CREATIVE MIND OF EMMANUEL SIMMS**

## CONTENTS

|   | Acknowledgments | 4 |
|---|---|---|
|   | Introduction | 6 |
| 1 | The Vision | Pg 11 |
| 2 | Perception | Pg 26 |
| 3 | Drive | Pg 43 |
| 4 | Check-in | Pg 60 |
| 5 | Always Deliver | Pg 77 |
| 6 | Stop Hiding | Pg 91 |
| 7 | Your Time is Now | Pg 106 |
|   | 7 Habits of Highly Creative People | Pg 115 |
|   | About the Author | Pg 118 |

# I GOT IT WHY NOT USE IT?

## ACKNOWLEDGMENTS

I wish to be the best role model for them I can be, and that means striving to improve myself every day. I am sorry if I don't constantly have everything together–but I commit I am doing my best for you. I love you all very much.

I'm sorry for not always having it together, Emmanuel Jr., Aubree, and Noah. As your father, each day I work hard to make sure I learn something new to teach and provide for you. I want you to know that I love you and I'm doing the best I can.

When I was younger, I always felt like I had to justify my existence. I differed from everyone else, and I didn't quite fit in. It was only when I found my purpose in life that I could truly be myself.

My purpose is to help others. I want to be there for those who are struggling, to offer my support and help them heal. I know I can make a difference in the lives of others and that motivates me.

I am grateful to my friends, fans, and family for understanding that I am a unique soul living to heal those of our community. Thank you for supporting me and allowing me to be who I am.

FROM THE CREATIVE MIND OF EMMANUEL SIMMS

# Introduction

Are you good at something? Do you have talent? Questions you should ask yourself before reading this book. On the next page, I want you to write them down. I want you to be the first person to give "you" a chance before you look for others to invest in you or help you. Let's get you into the habit of helping you. Self-support is something that will take you a long way.

Self-care is one of the most important things you can do for yourself. It's not selfish to take care of yourself–it's essential. When you take care of yourself, you're able to be there for others, too.

Here are some simple self-care tips that can help you get started:

1. Get enough sleep. Most people need around eight hours of sleep per night. Consider going to bed and waking up at the same time each day to help regulate your body's natural sleep rhythm.

## I GOT IT WHY NOT USE IT?

2. Eat healthy foods. Eating nutritious foods helps your body to function at its best. Include plenty of fruits, vegetables, and whole grains in your diet.

3. Exercise regularly. Exercise releases endorphins, which have mood-boosting effects. A moderate amount of exercise is the key to maintaining your mental health and well-being.

4. Take breaks when you need them. If you're feeling overwhelmed or stressed, take a few minutes to yourself to relax and rejuvenate. Take a hot bath, read your favorite book, or take a walk outdoors.

5. Connect with loved ones. Spending time with loved ones can help reduce stress and promote positive emotions. Whether you stay in touch via text, social media, or in person, quality time with those you care about is crucial for a healthy mind and body.

**FROM THE CREATIVE MIND OF EMMANUEL SIMMS**

Taking care of yourself is essential to living a happy and fulfilling life. By incorporating these simple self-care tips into your daily routine, you can improve your overall wellbeing. My point is, while you are living and able to do what you should do. If you have talents, why not use it? Gifts and talents aren't like roll over minutes. When you don't use, then you will lose them.

# I GOT IT WHY NOT USE IT?

## List of Gifts, Talents, and Specialties.

**FROM THE CREATIVE MIND OF EMMANUEL SIMMS**

# Chapter 1

## The Vision

## I GOT IT WHY NOT USE IT?

The children's book "The Three Little Pigs" talks about how each little pig builds their home. Their homes represent you. Each pig picked unique elements to build each home. One pig used a straw. If you have ever seen straw in person, you know it's thin and easily broken. The other pig created his house with furze sticks, twigs, and switches, another weak element that, with the right amount of pressure, can break. The third pig builds the house that you plan to be by the end of this book and builds his home with bricks. Dictionary says a brick is a block or a unit of ceramic material used in masonry construction. Typically, bricks stack together or laid as brickwork, using various kinds of mortar to hold the bricks together and make a permanent structure. Build your life with bricks so that you can live with a permanent structure. How do you do that? You start by taking your time, not rushing into the first thing, and asking questions about if this is what you want to do. Not like the other two pigs that used straw and twigs, because as soon as trouble came their way with a huff and a puff, everything they had built destroyed. Luckily, they had their brother to go to and stay in the house of a solid base.

## FROM THE CREATIVE MIND OF EMMANUEL SIMMS

See, we must think like the third pig. He didn't wait to see the other two make their mistakes. He knew from the beginning that there would be hardships that would come, storms that would grow. By not allowing himself to be afraid of what to come, but causes this set up an opportunity for him to help his two siblings.

You probably are wondering where I'm going with all of this? The title of the chapter says the vision, right? Well, let's look at the word vision for us to do that. We must be able to do what? To see! Vision is the sense of sight. On a spiritual experience, it conveys a revelation or a perception of something that does not exist or what you want to exist. See it, close your eyes, and see yourself where you want to be and then say it. People who believe in the rules of attraction suppose if they say they will have a good day, then they will. If they say I'm going to get a hundred dollars, then eventually they will, when the time is right. I'm not here to preach, but one Sunday I was in church. This was my first time in almost a year. This Sunday I felt moved by the music and the spirit that

## I GOT IT WHY NOT USE IT?

was in the room. During this time, I heard God tell me to give twenty-five dollars. I know it doesn't sound like a lot, but it's a lot when you only have twenty-eight in your pocket to get you through the week. Now I will not act like I didn't say God, you know this all I got? But I trusted him. I trusted his word, "Give, and it will give to you. A good measure, pressed down, shaken together, and running over, will pour into your lap. For with the measure you use, we measure it to you." Luke 6:38. True to his word, he always is. The next day, I got a call from my mentor telling me he had a gig for me and wanted to see if I could make it to the venue. I thought I would perform, to discover he wanted me to take pictures and shoot video. By the end of the night, we stopped at an ATM, and he gave me some money and if I ever held a stack of twenties in your hand. You can imagine I didn't feel the need to count because whatever it was, it was better than what I had in my pocket. He told me it was two hundred and eighty dollars. I responded I need to get out and give God some praise because by me being obedient, he took my twenty-five dollars and multiplied it by then and some. So, believing and seeing can lead you to the top so let's jot down your vision of where you want to be, then let's follow the rules of attraction for two weeks and call out what you want to do or what your needs

## FROM THE CREATIVE MIND OF EMMANUEL SIMMS

are and let it in to the air let's believe that you will get what you claim. Start your statement by saying I have, or I will demand, whatever it is you need or want.

# I GOT IT WHY NOT USE IT?

I Have… I Will…

**FROM THE CREATIVE MIND OF EMMANUEL SIMMS**

I Have… I Will…

## I GOT IT WHY NOT USE IT?

When you wake up for the next couple of weeks, I want you to grow your vision. See what you want and what you must do to get it. Earlier, I told myself I wanted to publish a book. Before the end of the year, I put this on a list of things I wanted to do. I created this list after my twenty-second birthday in February. I had never published a book before and did not know how to go about doing it. Doing some research and asked other local authors how they did it and how long it took. After getting all the info I needed, I admit I procrastinated, which most of us do. I waited all the way till September to man up and say I'm doing it. I wrote my first book now, feeling the hard part was done. Little did I know. Because I was being cheap, I let one of the English tutors at my school edit my book. The first day we set down, I thought this was going to be perfect. I let her take my book home to finish it, which she never did. I refuse to wait on her to finish the edit, so I published it as is. Knowing I stopped worrying about people thinking whatever they were going to think, and I just did it. The Rules of a Successful Failure is an edited version of my book. Now available on Audible and Amazon. That was all that went wrong when the books arrive, they were twice the size of a normal book and the fonts were huge, but I didn't let that stop me I still promoted my book and sold copies all over my school and workplace getting some positive feedback about the book besides the fact it had all the errors people felt the book was a good read.

Now I'm not telling you to go publish an unedited book, but you will never know how it feels to try unless you do it. This opened doors for me to publish my mother's first book of many. This showed me if I wanted, I could do it again and fix all the glitches that I ran across in the initial release of this book. But let's say I didn't try to. I waited for this person to edit my book and 2014 came around the corner. I would have just added this to the pile we all have of things we wish we could have or would have. No more. Let's break the chain.

# I GOT IT WHY NOT USE IT?

Let's stop putting things aside until things are perfect and let's play a game of life and death. If I do it, I live and if I don't; I die. Would you do it?

Today times have changed. We have just an equal chance at being anything that we want. It seems like the land of opportunity is living up to its name. If you say I want to start a T-shirt business, it's easy as one, three, two. Don't ask, but I'll tell you later why not one, two, three? There was a guy I knew who looked just like me. He was me and I am him. Spending so much money on getting custom shirts made in Iverson mall. having to buy the shirt and pay for each design I put on the shirt. I spent about three hundred dollars a month in this store buying and pressing shirts till I watched them make the shirts. Seeing what machine they used and asking what paper they used. Next couple of months I stopped visiting this place. I started saving and researching the price of the heat press machine they used, and I found one. The price of the machine was equivalent to what I spent in a month. Then I remembered how my grandmother used to go to the 5th street market and buy things wholesale. What I remember most is how in one store she went to a lot where they had shirts. So, I asked my mom where this place was, found it, and purchased a few dozen shirts which were about a buck fifty each. Guess you can say I came off, right? Well, it was still one thing I needed to make my business complete. I needed that excellent paper used to make the best quality of work. I went back to this store and got more info on the machine. Of course, the guys were asking why they haven't seen me in a while. I eventually told them I had purchased my heat press machine and wouldn't be needing to come there anymore for their services. I found another later, a great place to order the paper, and I was ready to open the shop. Before I put the word out that people can come and order, I wanted to get familiar with the machine myself. I practiced on old shirts until I felt confident that I was ready to try on one of my extra shirts, and then I did. This story brings me proof of the fact you can't be afraid to get out and try. Taking my time to learn every detail. Saw the problem that I was spending too much on something I could do myself. I am

## I GOT IT WHY NOT USE IT?

using my sense of vision to see what I needed, went out and got what I needed, and started my t-shirt business in a matter of months, and it's that easy. Find a goal, plan, and see it through. On the next page, I want you to write what it is you want and what you need to do to get it. Write what elements they will need to build your goal and go get it. That's a challenge and I want to hear what you did after this.

**FROM THE CREATIVE MIND OF EMMANUEL SIMMS**

Things you need to reach Your Goal

**I GOT IT WHY NOT USE IT?**

Things you need to reach Your Goal

# FROM THE CREATIVE MIND OF EMMANUEL SIMMS

Growing up, I always thought it was normal to work to get what I want. This was something that I learned about living in Virginia. being raised in several places. My family moved around a lot, but in my life, I learned the ropes. Living in Chesterfield, I got to see the fast light of the country part of Virginia. Where people sold and used drugs, which I had seldom seen growing up. I live a few blocks from Virginia State University. During my freshman year of middle school, I spent a lot of time on campus. I watched the college kids sell anything they could get their hands on. So, what I would do in the morning with the dollar my mom gave me for school or that I earned doing whatever I did? I would go into the store sitting at the top of the main street, buy a six-pack of strawberry rolls, then take it to school and sell them for a dollar each. When I got to my last treat, I doubled the price because the demand had risen. By the end of the week, I made about thirty to forty dollars. I sold anything I could get my hands on pencils and paper; I even hung out in the lost and found and would sell people their stuff that they lost. This was my starter lesson on supply and demand.

There are people in the world that make money off knowing what other people want or need. Statistics are the study of the collection, organization, analysis, interpretation, and presentation of data. It deals with all aspects of data, including the planning of data collection in terms of the design of surveys and experiments. Using the information gathered allows these researchers the advantage of knowing what you want, what you need, and how to get it to you. In your daily life, study yourself and your goal. Do you want to be a barber? Look around your neighborhood, see how many people you meet every day that need a haircut, then look at the people who already have nice haircuts. Ask them where they attend to get their hair cut. After you find a place that is the most popular in your area with the best cuts, you go in for a trip. By this time, you should already have the name of the best barber, where his chair I, is and how often he cuts. From the moment you walk in, you work, you talk; you ask questions. What school did this barber attend? How does he feel about the school? If you already have your barber's certification and you're just

## FROM THE CREATIVE MIND OF EMMANUEL SIMMS

looking for a job, find out who does the hiring, how much the monthly charge, and what the owner or manager looks for in a stylist.

Now you are at the top barbershop in your area. You made friends with the best barber and have all the basic info to get your feet in the door. You know what school that they are training in this league of super barbers in your area and now you can become one yourself.

Take your vision to the next level. Do whatever it takes! Research! Relate! React! Three Rs you can use for just about any goal you are trying to reach. Apply these to your life. Research! Relate! React! With your children, spouse, or employer, see what they need to gain knowledge on the product/issue, connect the info you found to the situation at hand, and then react. Give it all you treat your goal like you would if someone harmed you or your closest relative. You can let your feelings affect you. You can ask yourself what if you must get up and force your dreams to come true? Never allow your vision to be stopped. Remember that pig with the brick house permanent structure?

# Chapter 2

Perception

# FROM THE CREATIVE MIND OF EMMANUEL SIMMS

Perception is reality. I never understood that until I finally found out that it was one hundred percent true. 2011 I got injured at work and had to go to the hospital. When I was at the hospital, I had a few words with the nurse about how upset I was about this happening. She took it into her own hands to put on the file that I was rude. A few months later, my boss pulled me aside and asked about this. I didn't deny it and that day was the first time I heard the statement that perception is reality.

After reading my file and finding out this info, he went to the store that I was working at and asked everyone I worked with what they thought of me. This opened doors I couldn't afford to be opened. By being a shift supervisor at such a

## I GOT IT WHY NOT USE IT?

young age, I noticed I left a blind spot visible. Many people had their own opinions about me, which people will have about you if they don't already. Some people felt since they had been with the company for so long, they should be a manager. Others believed I was too young to be a manager and why should they listen to someone ten years younger than them? My attitude in the hospital opened a door for my district manager to think I had anger management issues. The words on the paper written had changed this guy's perception of me. A year earlier, he came into KFC three days back-to-back, watching me. I was a shift supervisor. He said he loved my customer service and wanted to hire me to work for him. I didn't do well on the test to get the job, but he was so impressed about me being married so young and already a shift supervisor; he gave me a shot. Now you see how one person can change the opinion of someone who valued you with such brief words.

Now, by him asking other people if they saw me get upset or any signs of anger issues, it put my coworkers on an

**FROM THE CREATIVE MIND OF EMMANUEL SIMMS**

alert, especially the ones who had it out for me. Now if I showed any anger, they were calling him, trying to add fuel to this misunderstanding. We must ask ourselves how we want others to perceive us. How do we perceive ourselves? What is true in the middle of both perceptions? On the next two pages, I want you to write out your answers.

## How Do Others Perceive Me?

**I GOT IT WHY NOT USE IT?**

How Do Others Perceive Me?

**FROM THE CREATIVE MIND OF EMMANUEL SIMMS**

How Do I Perceive Myself?

**I GOT IT WHY NOT USE IT?**

How Do I Perceive Myself?

**FROM THE CREATIVE MIND OF EMMANUEL SIMMS**

Now we know how both parties and others view you. Let's find the medium. Let's see if we can control your image before they categorize us. How? Easy to find out how you want to be looked at and look the part.

You are the product; you are the first idea or image of your business and your goal that anyone is going to see. If you don't look at the part, how can they believe you can play the part? You ever wonder why people wear uniforms when you were in the high school play where you had to dress up because you wanted to see the entire vision?

## I GOT IT WHY NOT USE IT?

With my marketing company, I help brand you. I will make you change people's views. We set up this game of perception and we let the opinions grow from there. As a recording artist, I know people will buy into what they believe you spent in the making or what was and is being spent on it. Having professional photos, videos, and luxury studio quality will have your friends looking at you like an entirely new person. Perception's not lying, just controlling the way people see you.

Most females look down at a man's shoes when they initially introduced, then at his face and haircut. If one of the two is not on point or at least decent, their view of you may be that you don't take pride in yourself. If both are top-of-the-line fresh, they can act as gold diggers and think you have money to blow. This is all before they know your name. For my guys, give it a test run, go out and pursue a random woman and watch her closely. Watch as her eyes stroll down to your feet, then back up so fast. In a matter of seconds, perception birthed.

## FROM THE CREATIVE MIND OF EMMANUEL SIMMS

Imagine this Caucasian man applying for a job. He puts his name down like everyone else who applied for the job. Before I go any further, I want to make it clear this isn't about racists, so let's eliminate that thought now. This Caucasian guy places his name on the application of Mohammed Kingston. You automatically think he's black and what else? And a Muslim, right? You as the employer don't discriminate and set Mohammed up for his interview. He meets all the requirements studied at Harvard, got his Ph.D., is a member of SGA, and has five years of being a manager in this field. It's eleven in the morning. You call for your eleven and this five-foot ten white male with blond hair and sandy brown eyes walks in, shakes your hand, and greets you.

What look do you see yourself making? It's as simple as that, as simple as your name. People will assume your name. Most people know my stage name is OverTyme Simms. What's your first opinion of my name when you hear it? The name is not an easy name to live up to. Because no matter the name, people still don't know what product they are going to

## I GOT IT WHY NOT USE IT?

get, but they know what to expect. Let's say you see my name posted up and you say I would love to see what OverTyme can do. You come to the show looking forward to whatever I do to be OVERTYME!!! You need to be all of that and more. After paying your money, you see it's worth it. I get on stage and own it. I perform with my heart into it, my soul becomes one with the sound and I live up to my name, Mr. Tyme, and a Half.

Perception rules the world and an old saying goes when in Rome, do as the Romans do. The media controls what you see. They serve information to you how they want you to receive it. They control the way we all perceive everything around us. Why not play by their rules and control how people view our business and view us as entertainers and business-minded individuals? You got it. Use it! Take a stand on what it is you love and believe and sell it. Selling it to everybody you see because one thing I have learned over time: everyone is a customer, and we are the product. Saying this means everywhere we go; we need to have our uniform on. We need

## FROM THE CREATIVE MIND OF EMMANUEL SIMMS

to have our best team with us. Our best-cooked meal. If you say you are a producer or a beat maker and don't have ten beats that you made ready to play, and Diddy walks in and says play something and you scramble to find a track or singers who says what you want me to sing. His perception of you is that you are not ready. Be prepared for anything good, bad, or worst. Be ready! Because it's easy to make people think negatively about you, but hard to make them think good. Perception is Reality.

What was the Peek of your Day?

## I GOT IT WHY NOT USE IT?

What was the Peek of your Day?

**FROM THE CREATIVE MIND OF EMMANUEL SIMMS**

*Another way to try...*

Parenting: parenting is difficult and can be ineffective if we don't break patterns before they get out of hand.

In most black homes, children are to be seen and not heard, staying in a child's place, or uneducated on the prices of their parents that they too one day will face.

## I GOT IT WHY NOT USE IT?

If you ever struggled at any point in your adult life and couldn't figure out why, there were no structures in places like the Brisker or the Bayu Family.

Instead, you had a system in place where your cousins compete, your uncles pass down trauma, normalizing highly sexual context and abuse of drugs and alcohol.

When passed down phrases like "give him here" when referring to a baby, perspective causes disconnection. Unable to understand why your relationships are not working, because the uneducated parent kept you uninformed.

The conversation never taught because you are used to being seen and not heard. When your words can't understand because this woman taught to listen and hear, but what you are saying, the recycled words from your dad, the clichés of your past.

## FROM THE CREATIVE MIND OF EMMANUEL SIMMS

All those accidentally on-purpose phrases that kept your parents in shackles now I'm being repeated to your child faces you don't even believe in phrases that were said to you and when your child Deerwood did, you reacted the same way that the person said it to you but instead of admitting that you were wrong you made a mistake you want to seem as perfect as the adults appear to you see you miss out on an opportunity to let your child know I miss spoke some things from my past. And I'm sorry what that does is it is your child to acknowledge one when he's wrong and to notice things that aren't fares that they are giving out to notice things to be picked up on the way but don't want to keep for the rest of the road it teaches them that just because I did something just a second ago doesn't mean it's right and just because the person who I did it to didn't know that it was wrong doesn't mean that it's OK to take advantage or to miss Lee's someone because of prior gain perception in fact when you do this you teach them pride by showing them it's OK to be wrong you open up a door to normalizing errors. This gives your child a chance to grow an opportunity to make mistakes, no feeling that they must be perfect, no delete they work too hard that they will be nothing to benefit from.

That if you don't practice reading soon, when you get older like me, you will struggle.

# Chapter 3

## Drive

**FROM THE CREATIVE MIND OF EMMANUEL SIMMS**

As I attended elementary school in Washington, DC, I remember standing outside every day before the students could enter the building. We had to recite a poem the poem titled "I AM SOMEBODY"

# I GOT IT WHY NOT USE IT?

I AM SOMEBODY

I am somebody

I am capable and lovable

I am teachable, therefore I can learn

I can do anything when I try

I will respect myself and others

I will be the best that I can be each day

I will not waste time because it is too valuable and

I am too precious and bright

I Am Somebody

We quoted this every day. I'm sure I didn't know what all these words meant, but it stuck with me as u got older. I have embedded this poem in my memory till today and is a prayer that I follow that will stick with me throughout my days.

## FROM THE CREATIVE MIND OF EMMANUEL SIMMS

By the time I was in middle school, I targeted again by motivating words in a song that played over the intercom "Wake Up Everybody", originally recorded by Harold Melvin & the Blue Notes. Right after the song finished, the staff member doing our morning announcement faithfully would say, "Make it a great day or not, the choice is yours." Even as a kid, I had this unforgettable drive fueled by what most people would consider a normal day at school. I took it as a push to be the best of me possible. I took it as a challenge every day to accomplish something new. An early memory I have while at an honor roll assembly was when my teacher presented me with my awards, but before I received the many awards that I got that day, she put me on the spot she quoted. This is my "I can't do it student". She had announced that I would come to her all the time saying, "I can't do it, I can't do it." Before each award I received that day, she recited, this is my I can't do it again. That day I got the most certificates given out which should be me even when I thought I couldn't do it. All it takes is to try. Trying is one of the hardest things in the world to do. Why? Because it's so many things that could go wrong, so

## I GOT IT WHY NOT USE IT?

many what if so many excuses, but if you try, you can do it. If you can think of it, you can do it.

Overcoming the fear isn't easy, but moves without applying pressure on the gas; yea sure it may move when it's not in the park, but does it get you where you need to go? In life, you need to be that. Get behind the wheel of your own life and put your feet on the gas as hard as you can and reach your goal. What motivates you? What discourages you? On the next two pages, I want you to write up a list of both. Then compare which side outweighs the other. Then cross out the things on the list of discouraging things you consider being small hold back and then I want you to succeed one of those things on the list motivates you and start being motivated once you cross out the things that discourage you, I don't want you to look back at them again. I don't want you to even listen to anyone else who says these words surround your life with all the positive and motivating things that will uplift and enrich your life.

**FROM THE CREATIVE MIND OF EMMANUEL SIMMS**

What motivates you?

## I GOT IT WHY NOT USE IT?

What motivates you?

# FROM THE CREATIVE MIND OF EMMANUEL SIMMS

What discourages you?

# I GOT IT WHY NOT USE IT?

What discourages you?

**FROM THE CREATIVE MIND OF EMMANUEL SIMMS**

For many years, I felt like I was stuck inside this vortex, where no matter what I did, I couldn't escape walking in circles. I used the school as an excuse. I guess you can say it

# I GOT IT WHY NOT USE IT?

was easier to get a master's in counseling than chase my dreams. Let's say life was a lot safer when I didn't know school was ending and here, I am, about to graduate. Yeah, right, let me self-sabotage and mess this up. Getting distracted can cause us to forget our drive. Running and running for years until there is nothing but fumes and smoke from the burnout. I picked an addiction up because who knew escaping was easier than getting into a car and driving to that open mic and performing your ass off? Or maybe you just need a reminder but have been too stubborn to listen to yourself anymore, because last time, I know it didn't go so well, but hear me out. When did it happen? The other day I'm looking in the mirror and I saw a guy who never gave up. I may have quit a few times, but I never gave up.

My youngest son will be one in two weeks from today and I promise you can't tell him anything. Not like a bad kid, but he knows what he wants, and not that any kids are bad. Just if they aren't mine, you better get them before they get kicked. But seriously, it looks like I'm getting tossed out of grad school

## FROM THE CREATIVE MIND OF EMMANUEL SIMMS

3 credits away from my master's because I let imposter syndrome eat me before selling my soul to public service and didn't write the easiest paper of my career. And if you're thinking if it was so easy, why didn't I write it, well I excuse you not, I forgot my drive. I forgot why I was even in school. And let's just say, did you throw that bucket of water on my universe? She did. She needed me to spend 3 long years grieving for my dad while in school, learning how to heal others for me to gain access to all the tools that were given to me at birth. It's like I was trying to put furniture together without the manual, completing the project just to see a couple of pieces laying over in the dark part of the living room. You can either go in and put those pieces away, hoping for the best until you break down and must go back later. Or you can undo the entire project now and rebuild using the manual. But most of us are lazy and will take the easier option, keep going and hope for the best.

The issue with that is that we are not furniture, that sits in a gloomy living room hoping for a companion to "add some

## I GOT IT WHY NOT USE IT?

light up on here" but we move and go, we jump, we bend, and we are everything but still. Imagine with me, it's the only way you will see this. You are being engineered, and a person building realizes they forgot to read the manual and two parts are missing. What if those two parts are your heart and soul? How are you going to live? This engineer then chooses the first option and waits until something goes wrong. Now you spend your entire life heartless and can't dance. If you wouldn't want anyone else handling you with this kind of care, why would you handle yourself?

But let's say you chose the latter and you remove all the parts going back to check the manual or as I would teach my first graders, go back, and look at the text. Going back allows you to explore the process again, so when you rebuild you know why this heart piece is so important, and how the soul needed to make sure Sundays are perfect by 5 pm. Remember, we are building for foundation, leaving no spaces, no spaces because of gaps, allowing entry of the unwanted and all its friends. The next page is a list of affirmations. Affirmations are

**FROM THE CREATIVE MIND OF EMMANUEL SIMMS**

a neat tool to add to your lunchbox on this journey of life. This one is for resilience since this chapter is all about the drive. Resilience is the ability to always recover from any form after being destroyed. I am resilient and so are you.

## I Are Resilient Affirmations

- I have a history of surviving.
- I can defeat all the odds.
- Doubt has no hold over me.
- I easily manage change.
- The life I want is the life I deserve.
- My possibilities are endless.
- I will write my story.
- I might bend, but I will never break.
- A scar is just additional armor.
- A setback is simply a detour.
- No matter what, I will keep.
- I release everything that weighs me down.
- I release everything that holds me back.
- Disruption does not last forever.
- I believe in my power.
- The universe supports my path.
- I have the strength and wisdom I need to handle anything.
- I can seek help when I need it.
- I can adapt.
- The universe lights my way.

## Write Ten Affirmations

**FROM THE CREATIVE MIND OF EMMANUEL SIMMS**

**Write Ten Affirmations**

# I GOT IT WHY NOT USE IT?

**FROM THE CREATIVE MIND OF EMMANUEL SIMMS**

## Reflection

I want you to use the next couple of pages to reflect. You can doodle, write, or paint if you like, but it's recommended you take a break, pause if you are listening to do, and just take time to be. I challenge you to not take in any more information to allow your brain to breathe. So, loosen that headband and allow yourself to be yourself.

# Chapter 4

## Check-in

# FROM THE CREATIVE MIND OF EMMANUEL SIMMS

I debated if I should have ended the last chapter by saying the actual work starts soon or is coming up, but I wanted you to take a chill because the actual work starts now. And if you jumped ahead, I tried to give you a break. This section is about doing the work and an introduction to Burnout.

For many people, the term "burnout" conjures up images of working long hours at a high-stress job. But burnout can happen to anyone, in any line of work. It's not just about working too hard. A combination of factors caused burnout, including a lack of control, unrealistic expectations, and a lack of support.

When you're burned out, you may feel exhausted, hopeless, and resentful. You may find it hard to concentrate or sleep, and you may get sick more often. If you're experiencing any of these symptoms, it's important to act.

There are three key steps to recovering from burnout:

1. Recognize the signs.

2. Change your lifestyle and work habits.

3. Seek professional help if necessary.

If you're struggling with burnout, reach out for help. There are many resources available to you, and with the right support, you can get back on track.

Burnout is a state of physical, emotional, and mental exhaustion that prolonged or unmanaged stress can cause. It's important to know the signs of burnout so you can identify it in yourself or in someone you know. Symptoms of burnout include fatigue, headaches, and trouble sleeping. Irritability, anxiety, and depression are the emotional signs. Mental signs include feeling overwhelmed, difficulty concentrating, and memory problems.

If you're experiencing any of these signs, it's important to take a step back and assess your situation. Are you taking on too much? Do you need to take a break? Are you doing something you're passionate about?

It's also important to talk to someone about what you're going through. Burnout can be overwhelming and it's important to have a support system. If you don't have one, there are plenty of resources available online or through your local community. No one deserves to experience burnout. If you or someone you know is struggling, reach out for help.

Burnout is a genuine phenomenon that can affect anyone. It's important to be aware of the signs and symptoms of burnout so that you can prevent it from happening to you.

Feelings of exhaustion, cynicism, and feelings of inadequacy characterize burnout. If you're experiencing any of these symptoms, it's important to take a step back and assess your current situation. Are you taking on too much? Are you not taking enough time for yourself?

There are a few key things you can do to prevent burnout:

1. Set realistic goals for yourself and your team.
2. Make sure you're taking regular breaks, both during the day and on weekends.
3. Take time for yourself outside of work, whether that means pursuing a hobby or taking a vacation.
4. Make sure you're communicating openly with your team and your supervisor.
5. Seek professional help if you feel you're struggling to cope.

Burnout is 100% preventable if you're willing to take the steps. Don't let yourself felt overwhelmed and exhausted. Take care of yourself and your career will thank you for it.

## FROM THE CREATIVE MIND OF EMMANUEL SIMMS

Now that we understand what burn out as we can get to the work if you're not aware of the enemy, it'll get you every time.

It's estimated that we humans experience fear around 365 times a day. That's once for every waking minute. And for many of us, fear can feel like it's paralyzing. We can be afraid of the future, of what other people think of us, of failure, of success, of change.

Fear is a normal and necessary emotion. It's what kept our ancestors alive when faced with predators and other dangers. But when fear takes over our lives, it can become a problem.

So, how do we deal with fear?

The first step is to realize it. Once we're aware of our fear, we can deal with it.

## I GOT IT WHY NOT USE IT?

There are many ways to deal with fear. Some people like to face their fears head-on. Others prefer to take a more gradual approach. And there's no right or wrong way to do it.

One way to deal with fear is to think about what's the worst that could happen. And then realize that, in most cases, the worst-case scenario isn't that bad.

Another way to deal with fear is to take small steps. For example, if you're afraid of public speaking, you could start by speaking in front of a small group of friends. Or if you're afraid of change, you could start by changing your life.

The most important thing is to not let fear stand in your way. Fear is the enemy, but if you're not aware of the enemy, it'll get you every time. So don't let fear hold you back from living your life to the fullest. There's no doubt that inner fears can be crippling. But there are ways to face them and even overcome them. Here are a few tips:

1. Understand what your fears are. This may seem obvious, but it's important to take some time to really think

about what scares you. What are the consequences of those fears? When you clearly understand your fears, you can work on addressing them.

2. Don't be afraid to ask for help. Whether it's talking to a therapist or counselor, or even just confiding in a trusted friend or family member, taking the first step to reaching out for help can be incredibly helpful.

3. Create a plan. Once you know what your fears are, it's time to think about how you can address them. What are some small steps you can take to face your fears? Having a plan can help you feel more in control and may make facing your fears feel less daunting.

4. Take your time. Remember that you don't have to face your fears all at once. Breaking the process down into smaller, more manageable steps can help you make progress without feeling overwhelmed.

5. Be patient with yourself. Facing your fears can be a long and difficult process. But it's important to remember that

# I GOT IT WHY NOT USE IT?

everyone moves at their own pace. Give yourself time and grace as you work through this process.

## What Are Your Fears?

**FROM THE CREATIVE MIND OF EMMANUEL SIMMS**

**What Are Your Fears?**

## I GOT IT WHY NOT USE IT?

After you've wrapped your fears, it's time to get to work. Your work won't do itself. But don't worry, you can handle it. You're tough and you're brave. So go out there and show the world what you're made of.

We all have fears. Some of us are afraid of failure. Others are afraid of success. But we all must face our fears and do the best we can.

So don't be afraid to work hard. Don't be afraid to put yourself out there. You can do it. I believe in you.

Now go out there and conquer the world. You got this!

**FROM THE CREATIVE MIND OF EMMANUEL SIMMS**

Self-improvement can feel like a daunting task, but it doesn't have to be. By taking small steps and focusing on your inner thoughts and feelings, you can make actual progress.

Start by taking a few moments each day to reflect on how you're feeling. Are you happy with your current situation, or are there areas that you'd like to improve? Once you've identified areas you'd like to work on, it's time to take action.

Pick one area that you'd like to focus on and set a goal. For example, if you want to improve your self-esteem, your goal might be to accept compliments from others. Or, if you want to be more confident, your goal might be to speak up more often.

Once you have a goal in mind, start taking steps to reach it. This might mean attending a self-improvement class, reading positive affirmations, or practicing visualization exercises. Remember, it's important to focus on your inner thoughts and feelings as you work towards your goal.

## I GOT IT WHY NOT USE IT?

By taking small steps and focusing on your inner thoughts and feelings, you can make actual progress in your self-improvement journey.

Self-improvement is a lifelong journey. It's something that you work on every day, bit by bit. And it starts with taking care of yourself, both physically and mentally.

Eating right, exercising, and getting enough sleep are all important for keeping your body healthy. But your mental health is just as important. Take time each day to relax and de-stress. Talk to a friend or therapist if you're feeling overwhelmed.

It's also important to set goals for yourself and work towards them. Whether it's getting a promotion at work or running a marathon, having something to strive for can help keep you motivated.

Finally, don't be too hard on yourself. Everyone makes mistakes. Learn from them and move on. Be proud of the progress you've made and keep.

# FROM THE CREATIVE MIND OF EMMANUEL SIMMS

In conclusion, conquer your fears and work on yourself from the inside out. You are not what you think you are; you are what you do. Conquer your fears, and work on yourself from the inside out. You are not what you think you are - you are what you do.

For facing our fears, we often think that we need to work on ourselves from the outside in. We think we need to change our circumstances or the surrounding people to feel better. But we need to work on ourselves from the inside out.

The first step is to realize our thoughts and feelings. What are we thinking and feeling when we face our fears? Do we believe that we're not good enough or that we'll never be able to overcome our challenges? Once we realize our thoughts and feelings, we can challenge them.

Instead of thinking, "I'm not good enough," try thinking, "I can do this." Instead of thinking, "I'll never be able to overcome my challenges," try thinking, "I'm willing to face my challenges and I know I can overcome them."

## I GOT IT WHY NOT USE IT?

When we change our thoughts, we change our feelings. And when we change our feelings, we change our behavior. So instead of avoiding our fears, we can face them head on. The more we face our fears, the more they'll lose their power over us. And the more we conquer our fears, the more confident and capable we'll feel. So don't let your fears hold your back - start working on yourself from the inside out today.

**FROM THE CREATIVE MIND OF EMMANUEL SIMMS**

# Let Go Of Fear Affirmations

1. Whatever comes my way, I can handle it.
2. A setback will strengthen me.
3. I am powerful, and I am strong.
4. I am brave; I am courageous enough to take chances.
5. I can achieve anything I set my mind to.
6. With every passing day, my confidence grows.
7. I possess limitless abilities.
8. I deserve happiness.
9. I let go of stress, tension, and fear.
10. I always do my best.
11. I am grateful; I am strong.
12. I see happiness and hope when I look to the future.
13. It's easier to move forward in courage than in fear.
14. My dream is worth fighting for.
15. I have unconditional love for myself.
16. I never give up, I am resilient.
17. I have the courage to conquer fear.
18. The universe will protect me.
19. I am as determined as I am confident.
20. I am fearless; I am fierce.

# Chapter 5

Always Deliver

# FROM THE CREATIVE MIND OF EMMANUEL SIMMS

Do you remember when I said they call me OverTyme well, let's get into this next chapter. Always deliver, always deliver because your name your brand is on the line. We all have those people in our lives that seem to think that our time belongs to them. The expectations keep mounting until we don't even know who we're trying to please anymore. It's tough to manage, but it's important to remember that you have a say in how your time spent. You can't always make everyone happy, but you can put your own needs first and make sure that you're taking care of yourself.

When you present yourself to the world, you are effectively branding yourself. Whether you like it, people will judge you based on your appearance and how you carry yourself. Therefore, it's important to always put your best foot forward, especially if you're offering a service or commodity.

## I GOT IT WHY NOT USE IT?

Your brand reflects who you are, so make sure that it is something you're proud of. Take the time to cultivate a positive image and always be mindful of how you're being perceived. It takes effort to build an excellent reputation, but it only takes one mistake to lose it.

Be always professional and courteous and treat others with respect. Remember that first impressions matter, so make sure you're making the best one possible. It might seem like a lot of pressure, but if you focus on being the best version of yourself, you will stand out from the rest.

I started out in the music industry over 10 years ago, and ever since then I've been striving to live up to the name and brand of OverTyme. It's a lifestyle that I'm very passionate about, and I want to share it with as many people as possible. I believe that music has the power to change lives, and I'm dedicated to using my platform to spread that message. I'm so grateful to have such a loyal following, and I promise to always deliver the best possible music and performances for you all. Thank you for supporting me on this journey, it means the world to me.

I've been in the business for a long time, and I've seen a lot of things. I've seen the good, the bad, and the ugly. But one thing I always try to do is deliver the truth.

When I first started, I remember. I was young and idealistic. I thought I could change the world with my words. And in some ways, I think I did. But over time, I've learned that the business of journalism is not always about changing the world. Sometimes, it's just about telling the truth.

There will always be people who don't want to hear the truth. They don't want to believe that the world is imperfect. But it is. And it's our job as journalists to tell those stories.

## I GOT IT WHY NOT USE IT?

So, even though it's not always easy, we must keep delivering the truth. Because in the end, that's all that really matters. I'm hoping that being honest has a better effect on the future than it does in the present. I'm not sure if that's true, but I'm going to try it.

I'm not perfect, and I never will be. I'm human and I make mistakes. Sometimes I'm lazy, or I don't want to do something. But I'm trying to be better. I want to be honest with you because I think it's important. And I hope that by being honest, I can make the world a better place.

Of course, if believing in yourself is something you struggle with, this can seem like a tall order. Luckily, there are a few things you can do to help increase your confidence, or faith in yourself. And one of the best ways to start is by engaging in positive media. This would mean reading motivational books and listening to positive, upbeat music.

# FROM THE CREATIVE MIND OF EMMANUEL SIMMS

The road to success can be difficult, and if you face an especially tough challenge, it can seem like it is just easier to give up. Therefore, you need to have a little faith in yourself, because when you believe in yourself, you will know you can conquer anything, and you won't feel like giving up.

This may not seem like much, but think about it, if someone told you, THAT you could have whatever you wanted 50 times every morning, wouldn't you believe it? So put a few positive songs on a playlist and listen to it each morning. You may just surprised by how much it helps.

Once you have some faith in yourself, it's time to help it grow. You can do this by celebrating the small successes in your life, no matter how small they may be. Did you get out of bed on time? Did you spend less time on social media today? Whatever your success may, celebrate it! And don't let anyone tell you that any success is too small. This is a critical part to building and maintaining your newfound confidence in life. Another way to help this faith in yourself to grow is by documenting your achievements. Although this may sound difficult, we can easily accomplish this by keeping a journal which you write in it daily. Or maybe even just a vision board that you add pictures of your successes to as you go. Again, this is something that looks different to everyone, and you need to do what makes you feel confident yourself.

So now you have confidence in yourself, and you are probably wondering just how this will help you when you face a challenge. This is because when you know yourself and know the power that you must overcome difficulties, they won't scare you so much.

In life, there is no way that you can control the actions of others. You can only control the actions of yourself. And having faith in yourself means that criticism from others, something you may not control which could challenge you, won't be able to knock you off your path.

Besides just helping you overcome challenges, having faith in yourself will make it easier for you to take risks in your life which may benefit you in the long run. This is because you will be less scared of the unknown—as you know there is nothing out there which can knock you off your path.

Having faith in yourself can be difficult, but it is necessary if you are going to conquer challenges in your life. If you need to develop some faith in yourself, you can do so by listening to positive music and reading motivational media.

Then you can grow this faith by celebrating and documenting the achievements you conquer each day; in whatever way you find best. And before you know it, your newfound confidence will have you surviving any

# I GOT IT WHY NOT USE IT?

challenge which comes your way and taking additional risks which could change your life for the better.

Check in with yourself and see how you're feeling. Are you happy, sad, anxious, angry, or something else entirely? Pay attention to what your body is telling you. If you're feeling any negative emotions, take a few deep breaths and see if you can let them go. If you can't, that's okay. Just acknowledge them and move on. Negative emotions are a part of life, but they don't have to control you. If you can learn to recognize and release them, you'll be one step ahead of the game.

Welcome. Before you do anything else today, I want you to do a mental body scan. Check in with yourself and see how you're feeling. Then, read the following affirmation on resilience 10 times.

# FROM THE CREATIVE MIND OF EMMANUEL SIMMS

"I am resilient. My strength is powerful. I am capable. Whatever comes my way, I can handle it. I am safe. I am loved. I am supported. I am connected."

Take a few deep breaths and repeat the affirmation to yourself as many times as you need to. Remember, you are resilient. You are strong. You are capable. Whatever comes your way, you can handle it. You are safe. I love you. You have supported. You are very connected.

How was the affirmation exercise? Now do another body scan to see if your mood has changed.

## You Are Resilient Affirmations

1. I have a history of surviving.
2. I can defeat all the odds.
3. Doubt has no hold over me.
4. I easily manage change.
5. The life I want is the life I deserve.
6. My possibilities are endless.
7. I write my story.
8. I might bend, but I will never break.
9. A scar is just additional armor.
10. A setback is simply a detour.
11. No matter what, I will keep.
12. I release everything that weighs me down.
13. I release everything that holds me back.
14. Disruption does not last forever.
15. I believe in my power.
16. The universe supports my path.
17. I have the strength and wisdom I need to handle anything.
18. I can seek help when I need it.
19. I can adapt.
20. The universe lights my way.

**FROM THE CREATIVE MIND OF EMMANUEL SIMMS**

How was the affirmation exercise? Now do another body scan to see if your mood has changed. Use the next two pages to illustrate or just write how you are feeling in this space right now. So, take a few minutes to think about how you're feeling and then express that in whatever way you feel comfortable. There's no right or wrong way to do this. Just let your feelings flow onto the page.

# I GOT IT WHY NOT USE IT?

## How Do You Feel?

**FROM THE CREATIVE MIND OF EMMANUEL SIMMS**

**How Do You Feel?**

# Chapter 6

Stop Hiding

# FROM THE CREATIVE MIND OF EMMANUEL SIMMS

Don't hide, period. What does it mean to hide? To hide is putting others first. Most people go through life hiding their true selves. They put on a mask and pretend to be someone they're not. Why do they do this? Because they're afraid of what others will think or say about them. They're afraid of being rejected. But what if you didn't have to hide? What if you could be your true self, fearlessly? Well, you can. It's called manifesting.

Manifesting is the act of creating your reality. It's about claiming what you want and believing that you can have it. It's about knowing that you are worthy of good things and that you deserve to be happy. When you manifest, you let go of your fears and doubts. You step into your power, and you claim what you want. You will not allow no dark forces or anyone to stop you.

So if you're ready to manifest your dreams, here's what you need to do:

# I GOT IT WHY NOT USE IT?

1. Get clear on what you want. The first step to manifesting is to get clear on what you want. What do you want to achieve? What do you want to have? What do you want to experience? Get as specific as possible.

2. Believe that you can have it. The second step is to believe that you can have what you want. This may require some self-reflection. Do you believe you deserve good things? Do you believe that you're worthy of happiness? If not, why not? Write your answers and work on changing your beliefs.

3. Act. The third step is to act towards your goal. This doesn't mean that you must have everything figured out. It just means that you need to move in the right direction. Take small steps every day that will get you closer to your goal.

Manifesting is a powerful tool that can help you create the life you want. So don't be afraid to try it.

Careful not to manifest against yourself. For manifesting, some people may feel as though they are undeserving of what they desire. We can see this where someone's spouse may want to be an artist, but

## FROM THE CREATIVE MIND OF EMMANUEL SIMMS

takes on a supportive role because they feel their partner is more deserving of that path. This can be a difficult mindset to break free from, but it is important to remember that everyone is deserving of their dreams and goals. It is only through fearless manifestation that we can achieve our true potential.

In my career I spent a ton of rime in the shadows, hiding behind some celebrity or mentor who I felt if I built them, they would build me.

One thing I've learned is that is not always true. I built people to where they outgrew me. Where my work was taken for granted because I was available. You see people will treat you how you teach them to treat you. Many people in the entertainment industry find themselves in the shadows, hiding behind the celebrities or mentors they work with. Often, they feel that if they can build up these people, they will be successful themselves. However, this is not always the case.

Working in the shadows can be a very frustrating and unfulfilling experience. You may do all the work, but it is the celebrities or mentors who get all the credit. This can be especially disheartening if you feel you are not being recognized for your efforts.

If you find yourself in this situation, it is important to remember that you are not alone. Many people in the entertainment industry are in the same boat. The key is to build your own personal brand and to create your own opportunities. This way, you can step out of the shadows and into the spotlight.

If you spend your life manifesting yourself as a steppingstone that what you will be. When you give your power away your hide who is truly you. If we spend our lives trying to be someone else's steppingstone, we will never really get to know ourselves. We will be constantly giving our power away, hiding our true selves.

Our lives will be a series of betrayals, as we try to be what others want us to be instead of being our authentic selves. It is only when we are true to ourselves that we can find happiness and fulfillment. So let us not be afraid to be who we are and let us not waste our lives trying to be someone else's steppingstone.

## FROM THE CREATIVE MIND OF EMMANUEL SIMMS

One thing that I talk about in my book "The Rules of a successful failure" is the importance of mentors in my life. Mentors have had a tremendous impact on me, both to provide guidance and support, and to help me become the person I am today.

Without mentors, I would not have been able to achieve the level of success that I have. They have helped me to develop my skills and knowledge, and to grow as a person. I am very grateful for their help and support.

However, I have also become dependent on their presence. I have got used to seeking approval from others, and this can be a hindrance to my success. I need to learn to trust my judgment and to stand on my own two feet.

Mentors have been a valuable part of my life, and I am grateful for their help. However, I need to learn to be independent if I am to truly succeed. I can remember a time when I would take rejections from editors personally. It felt like they were rejecting me as a person, rather than just my work. I would obsess over what I could have done differently and berate myself for not being good enough.

# I GOT IT WHY NOT USE IT?

Thankfully, I realized that this was not a healthy way to think, and that I needed to change my perspective. I saw rejections as simply a part of the publishing process. They didn't reflect on my worth as a person or writer, and I shouldn't take them to heart.

Now, when I receive a rejection, I simply move on. I know that there are other editors out there who will appreciate my work, and I don't waste time dwelling on those who don't. This has made the publishing process much more enjoyable, and has allowed me to focus on my writing rather than on the rejections. I wasn't paying for studio time directly so their approve was important if I was going to get my music out. I never thought that my music would never see the light of day. Years passed by with no success as I pushed back projects. Finally, I took matters into my own hands and pay for studio time myself. This way, I could release my music without having to get approval from anyone else. It was a risk, but it was one that I will take.

# FROM THE CREATIVE MIND OF EMMANUEL SIMMS

Thankfully, it paid off and my music is now out there for the world to hear. It feels amazing to have people listen to my music and to know that all of my hard work has paid off. If I had listened to the naysayers, my music would still hidden away, gathering dust. But now, it's out there for people to enjoy, and that's all that matters It's been a tough year. Rejection after rejection has taken its toll. I've felt hopeless, like I'm not good enough. But amid all this darkness, I've found myself.

This journey of self-discovery hasn't been easy. Every day feels like a battle. But I'm fighting–for myself, for my future. I refuse to give up. Because I know I am worth it. I am worth the fight.

I'm not sure when it happened, but at some point I stopped enjoying making music and taking photos. Life felt uninspiring, and I was no longer grateful for the gifts that I had been given. Thankfully, I realized that this was a temporary feeling and that I could choose to change my perspective.

## I GOT IT WHY NOT USE IT?

Now, I am grateful for each day that I get to wake up and create. Music and photography are my passion and I am determined to never lose sight of that. No matter what life throws my way, I will always find the beauty and inspiration in it. Thank you for being here with me on this journey.

To those of you who have been blessed with much, I say to you, that you have a responsibility to give back. It is not enough to simply live your life and enjoy your blessings. You must also share your blessings with others.

Think of all the people who are less fortunate than you. Think of all the people who are struggling just to get by. Now think of what you can do to help them. It doesn't have to be anything big or dramatic. Sometimes the simplest acts of kindness can make the biggest difference. So I urge you to reach out and help those who need it. Share your blessings with the world and make a difference in the lives of others.

Your gifts are your responsibility. No one can take them away from you, and no one can give them to you. You are the only one who can control your gifts. Use them wisely and they will be a great blessing in your life.

### Know You Can Handle Anything

A major part of trusting yourself is having the self-confidence to know that you've got this handled. Because fear of the unknown or the future will only breed more fear and make you ill prepared for what is coming.

If you struggle with your self-confidence, take a moment to look back at all you have accomplished, giving yourself a pat on the back for having come this far in life. You can also develop a positive affirmation for yourself, and when you have difficulty knowing your own abilities, repeat the affirmation to yourself to boost your self-confidence.

Now that you know you can handle anything, you can go towards the future without fear, because just deciding this alone can help prepare you for anything life has to throw at you. And chances are, when you face something difficult, it won't seem so difficult after all, and you'll quickly be able to conquer the new challenge you face.

# I GOT IT WHY NOT USE IT?

Overall, trusting yourself to do the right thing in every situation can be difficult, especially if you struggle with self-confidence. But if you want to be successful in life, this trust in yourself is absolutely necessary, otherwise you'll just repeat the same mistakes repeatedly. So, decide to change your life and decide to trust yourself and your decisions today, no matter what life may throw your way.

# FROM THE CREATIVE MIND OF EMMANUEL SIMMS

**Do you believe you deserve good things? Do you believe that you're worthy of happiness? If not, why not? Write your answers and work on changing your beliefs.**

# I GOT IT WHY NOT USE IT?

**Do you believe you deserve good things? Do you believe that you're worthy of happiness? If not, why not? Write your answers and work on changing your beliefs.**

FROM THE CREATIVE MIND OF EMMANUEL SIMMS

## Trust Yourself That Whatever Happens, You'll Handle It Affirmations

1. I trust my capabilities.
2. I believe in my intuition.
3. I am open to guidance and trust myself to choose wisely.
4. I am a safe person to trust.
5. I am a safe person to follow.
6. I am a safe guide.
7. I believe in myself.
8. I am worthy of trust.
9. I own my choices.
10. I own my decisions.
11. I listen to my intuition.
12. I can share my true self.
13. I possess all the wisdom I need.
14. I am aware; I am grounded; I am ready.
15. I can deal with difficult things.
16. I am walking the right path; my course is obvious.
17. I am safe; I am well.
18. Love, happiness, and peace live within me.
19. My inner voice is loud, confident, and clear.
20. I have the courage to be who I am.

# I GOT IT WHY NOT USE IT?

**How Do You Trust yourself?**

Of course, trusting yourself is easier said than done. According to Psychology Today, the best way to trust yourself is to start by relaxing and letting go of the small things that bother you in life. Instead, focus on the big picture and learn to treat yourself with kindness instead of resentment and anger. Next, you need to learn to see yourself clearly, and learn to let go of the criticism of others you may be internalizing. Because the only opinion of you that matters, is the one that you hold for yourself.

When you are working to let go of the criticism that you may keep tucked away in your mind, it's helpful to remember that people are often critical of you when they aren't happy with themselves or their own life.

And someone may have criticized you because they weren't happy with them, not because they had anything against you. Once you realize this, you will find it is much easier to let go of the things people have said and trust your own positive evaluation of yourself.

**FROM THE CREATIVE MIND OF EMMANUEL SIMMS**

# Chapter 7

## Your Time is Now

# I GOT IT WHY NOT USE IT?

Now is the time to take your career to the next level. With hard work and dedication, you can achieve your goals and reap the rewards that come with success. Let nothing stand in your way - now is your time to shine.

It's time to face life and take what is yours. No more hiding, no more fear, no more excuses. You've been ready this entire time and if you needed someone to tell you, I'm here to tell you got this. I can't wait to see what you've become. It's time to step out into the world and show everyone what you're made of. It's time to shine.

We've all been on a journey of self-improvement in our lives. Whether we're trying to lose weight, quit smoking, or simply be happier, we're always looking for ways to improve ourselves. And while there's nothing wrong with that, sometimes we need to do the work instead of just reading about it or talking about it.

For example, if we're trying to lose weight, we need to exercise and eat healthy, not just read about it or talk about it. And if we want to be happier, we need to do things that make us happy, not just read about it or talk about it. It's easy to get caught up in the idea of self-improvement and forget that it takes actual work to make it happen.

So, if you're on a journey of self-improvement, remember to do the work. It might be hard but it's worth it. And you'll be glad you did it when you reach your goals.

Looking back on who I was just a few years ago, it's hard to believe how far I've come. I remember being so lost, not knowing who I was or what I wanted to become. But thanks to this book, I could sit down

# I GOT IT WHY NOT USE IT?

and really think about who I am and what I want to achieve.

The time is now to pursue your dreams. Don't wait for someone else to give you permission or approval to go after what you want in life. You have everything you need to get started right now.

Don't let anyone tell you you can't achieve your dreams. You have the power to create your own reality. Act now and go after what you want with everything you've got. The time is now!

Now, I know exactly who I am and what I want to do with my life. I'm no longer lost but have a clear sense of purpose. This book helped to help me figure out who I am, and I'm forever grateful for that.

This book was extremely helpful in allowing me to draw and write out who I am and what I want to become. The ability to see my thoughts and feelings visually was very beneficial in understanding myself better. I appreciated the tone of voice throughout the book; it was informative and allowed me to process the information more effectively. Overall, this was an excellent resource in exploring my identity and I would recommend it to anyone seeking self-discovery.

It is often said that life is too short to wait around, and this is certainly true. If you wait too long to live your life, you might die without ever having truly lived.

Of course, not that you should recklessly throw caution to the wind. Living life to the fullest doesn't mean being careless. It simply means making the most of every moment, pursuing your dreams and doing what makes you happy.

Don't wait until it's too late to live your life. Carpe diem!

## I GOT IT WHY NOT USE IT?

In these uncertain times, it is important to remember that we all have something special to offer. We all have a light to carry that can make a difference in the world.

When faced with challenges, it's difficult to realize that we carry inside of us. But it is important to remember that we all could overcome adversity and make a positive difference in the world.

No matter what life throws our way, we must never give up on ourselves or our ability to make a difference. We all have the power to overcome any obstacle and bring our light to the world.

Today, it is easy to get lost in the hustle and bustle of everyday life. Someone constantly bombarded us with messages telling us what we should do, what we should buy, and who we should be. It's no wonder that so many people feel overwhelmed and stressed out all the time!

But what if I told you that there is a way to reduce the stress in your life and manifest your dreams? And it starts with you!

The key to manifesting your dreams is to change your mindset. Instead of focusing on all the things that are wrong in your life, or all the things you don't have, start focusing on what you DO have, and what you WANT to have. It sounds simple, but it's not always easy. Our minds are powerful, and often we get caught up in negative thinking patterns that can be hard to break free from.

But if you will put in the work and change the way you think about yourself and your life, you can absolutely manifest your dreams!

Start by Visualizing what you want. See it in your mind's eye as clearly as possible. Feel the feelings

# I GOT IT WHY NOT USE IT?

that you would feel if you had already achieved your goal.

Then, act steps towards your goal. Even if you don't know exactly how you're going to achieve it, trust that it will happen, and take steps in faith. Believe in yourself and know that you are worthy of achieving your dreams. Start today and see what happens!

**FROM THE CREATIVE MIND OF EMMANUEL SIMMS**

# Have Faith in Yourself to Survive Affirmations

1. I embrace my self-worth.
2. I support myself in the effort to achieve my goals.
3. There is nothing I cannot do.
4. I manifest love, health, and success.
5. Success does not define my self-worth.
6. I manifest success with my talents.
7. I am valuable.
8. Mistakes help me grow; I will survive them.
9. I am brimming with enthusiasm and confidence.
10. Change helps me grow; I embrace it.
11. I am courageous, I will live courageously.
12. I feel empowered when I face my fear.
13. I release all the pain from my past.
14. I will persist until I am clear.
15. Fear doesn't overwhelm me; I push through it.
16. My future is bright, I will endeavor for it.
17. I am worth fighting for.
18. My accomplishments are mine, and I am proud.
19. I am filled with beauty and strength.
20. Every day is an opportunity to succeed.

# I GOT IT WHY NOT USE IT?

*Creativity is a habit. Just like any other habit, it can be learned and developed. The 7 habits of highly creative people are:*

1. Be persistent: Highly creative people are not afraid of failure. They understand that failure is a part of the creative process and are persistent in their efforts to achieve their goals.

2. Be passionate: Highly creative people are passionate about their work. They have a strong desire to create and are always looking for new ways to express their ideas.

3. Be open-minded: Highly creative people are open to new ideas and experiences. They will experiment and take risks.

4. Be flexible: Highly creative people are flexible in their thinking. They can see the world from different perspectives and are open to change.

5. Be intuitive: Highly creative people trust their intuition. They can listen to their inner voice and follow their gut instincts.

6. Be self-disciplined: Highly creative people are self-disciplined. They can focus on their work and maintain their creative output.

7. Be positive: Highly creative people maintain a positive outlook on life. They believe in their ability to create and are always looking for the silver lining.

# I GOT IT WHY NOT USE IT?

## ABOUT THE AUTHOR

Emmanuel Simms is an American writer who is best known for his book The Rules of a Successful Failure. In his writing, he explores social issues such as race and discrimination within minority communities. Simms has a professional tone in his writing, which allows him to explore these difficult topics in a way that is both informative and relatable for his readers.

Simms grew up in a low-income, inner-city neighborhood. He witnessed firsthand the effects of discrimination and poverty on minority communities. This shaped his view of the world and inspired him to write about these issues in his books. In The Rules of a Successful Failure, Simms uses his personal experiences to explore what it takes to overcome adversity. He offers readers a unique perspective on the challenges faced by minorities in society and provides valuable advice on how to overcome them.

Simms' writing is important because it offers a rare look into the lives of minority communities. His insights can help readers to better understand the

# FROM THE CREATIVE MIND OF EMMANUEL SIMMS

difficulties faced by these groups, and can provide hope to those who are struggling to overcome them.

Made in the USA
Columbia, SC
15 July 2023